THE CONSTELLATION AQUARIUS

SIERRA WILSON

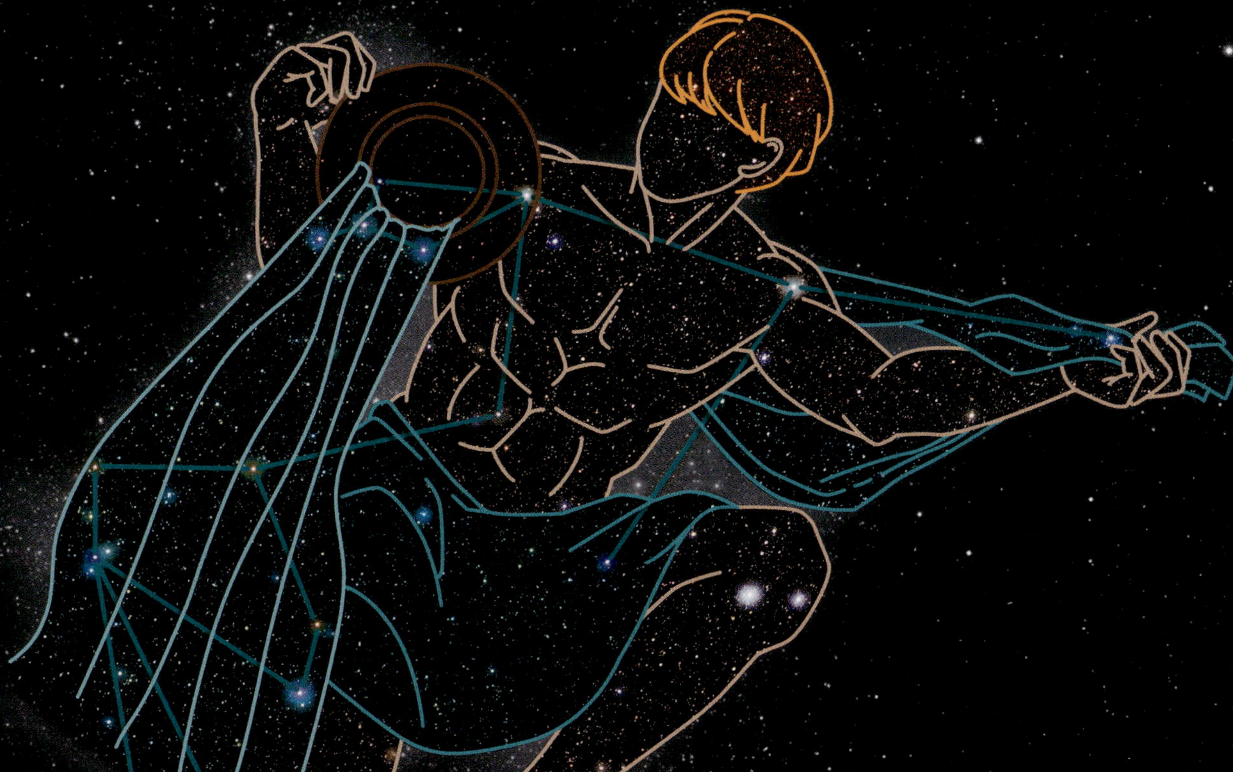

Published by The Child's World®
800-599-READ • www.childsworld.com

Photography Credits
Photographs ©: Shutterstock Images, cover (illustration), cover (background), 1 (illustration), 1 (background), 2 (illustration), 2–3, 5, 6 (illustration), 14, 24, 27, 28; E. Slawik/NSF/AURA/M. Zamani/NOIRLab, cover (constellation), 1 (constellation), 2 (constellation), 6 (constellation), 29; NASA, 8; M. Meixner and T. A. Rector/NOIRLab, 9; Tayfun Coskun/Anadolu/Getty Images, 10; ESO, 11 (galaxy); Natykach Nataliia/Shutterstock Images, 11 (atom); Natalia Mikhalchuk/Shutterstock Images, 13; Wikimedia Commons, 17; Michelangelo Maestri/Smithsonian, 18; Natalia Hubbert/Shutterstock Images, 21; Amanda Lewis/iStockphoto, 23; Design elements from Shutterstock Images

ISBN Information
9781503875777 (Reinforced Library Binding)
9781503876194 (Portable Document Format)
9781503876811 (Online Multi-user eBook)
9781503877313 (Electronic Publication)

LCCN 2025938257

Printed in the United States of America

ABOUT THE AUTHOR

Sierra Wilson is the author of several books for young readers. Sierra holds an MFA in creative writing and formerly worked as an English teacher. She is an Aquarius herself and loves studying the stars. Sierra grew up learning astronomy with her father and now passes on a love of constellations to her own children. She currently lives in Alberta, Canada, with her family.

TABLE OF CONTENTS

CHAPTER ONE

The Constellation Aquarius

For thousands of years, humans have looked up at the night sky. They saw the bright, shining lights above them. They wondered what the lights meant and where they came from. Today, scientists know that stars are giant balls of hot gas. But before this discovery, many cultures created their own stories about the stars. They often looked for shapes and patterns in the stars. These shapes are called constellations.

One well-known constellation is Aquarius. It is also known as the Water Bearer. Aquarius looks like a person pouring water from a jug. Aquarius is one of the International **Astronomical** Union's 88 official constellations. These official constellations are used to describe the location of objects in the night sky.

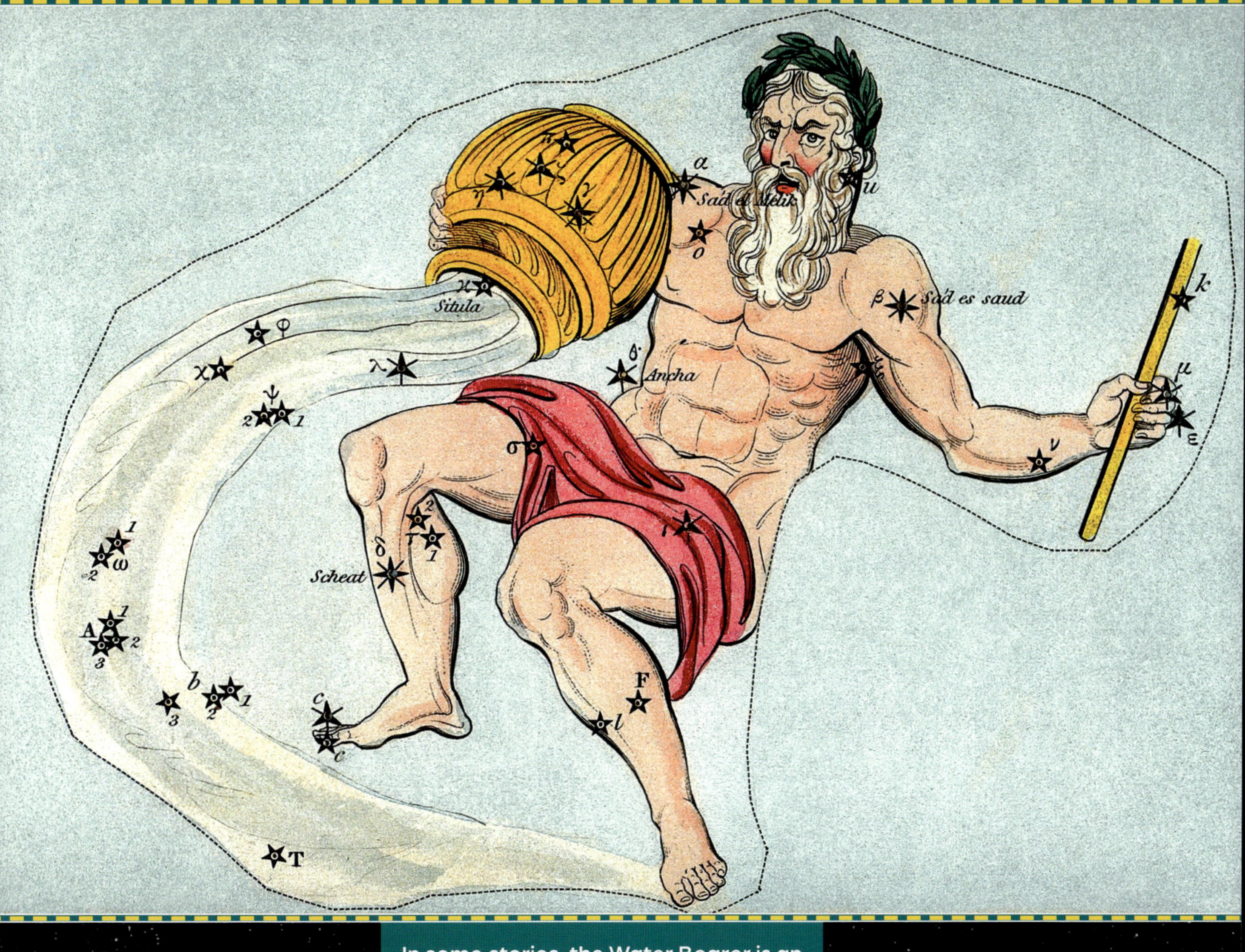

In some stories, the Water Bearer is an old man. In other stories, he is young.

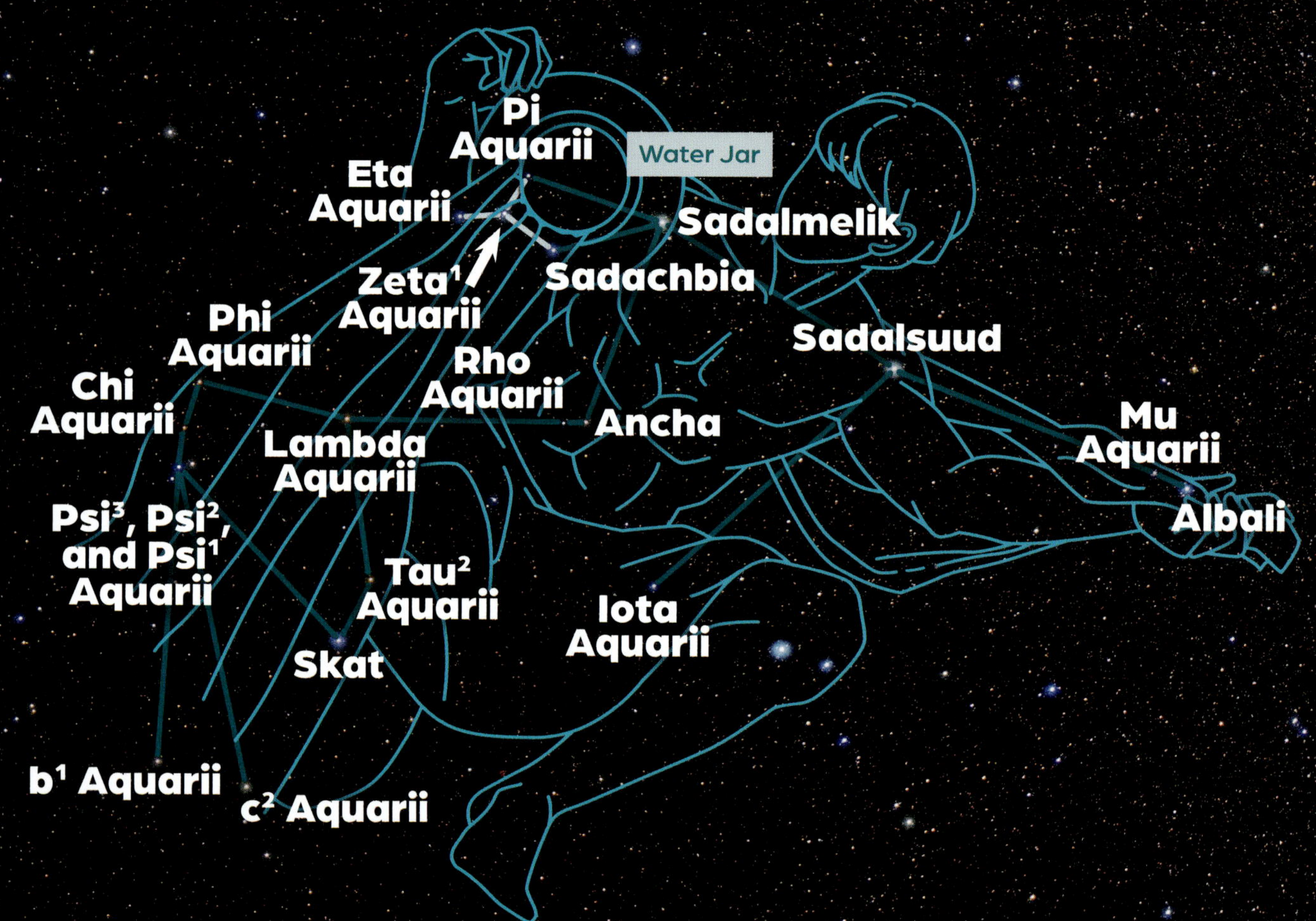

People include different stars in Aquarius's outline. This outline comes from the International Astronomical Union and *Sky & Telescope*.

Aquarius is one of the oldest known constellations. It is also one of the largest. Although Aquarius is large, it can be difficult to see. This is because the stars in Aquarius are not very bright. The brightest star in Aquarius is Sadalsuud (sad-ull-suh-OOD). This star's name comes from Arabic. It means "luckiest of the lucky." The constellation's second-brightest star is Sadalmelik (sad-ull-MEH-lihk). Its name means "lucky one of the king." Next to Sadalmelik is a small group of stars. They appear to form the letter Y. This region of Aquarius is an asterism known as the Water Jar. An asterism is a group of stars that is not an official constellation.

Aquarius is also home to other objects. Globular clusters are large groups of stars that are packed tightly together. They can have tens of thousands or even millions of stars. One globular cluster in Aquarius is Messier 2, or M2. It was the first globular cluster to be added to the Messier catalog. Astronomer Charles Messier started this list of deep-sky objects in the 1700s. The complete list contains 110 objects.

There are more than 150,000 stars in M2. This picture of M2 uses both visible light, which humans can see, and infrared light, which humans cannot see.

The Helix Nebula is famous for looking like an eye. Some people call it the Eye of God Nebula.

Aquarius is also home to **nebulae**. One is the Saturn Nebula. This nebula is named after the planet Saturn. This is because its gassy shape looks like a planet with rings. It is one of the brightest nebulae. Another nebula in Aquarius is the Helix Nebula. This is one of the closest nebulae to Earth.

METEOR SHOWERS

Meteor showers can also be seen within Aquarius. A meteor is space **debris** that has entered Earth's **atmosphere**. A meteor burns as it moves through the atmosphere. Meteors are sometimes called "shooting stars." A meteor shower occurs when many meteors appear in the sky at once. Meteor showers are named for the constellation the meteors seem to come from. The Eta Aquarids shower is best seen in late April into May every year. It appears to come from Aquarius.

A photographer in California captured Eta Aquarid meteors.

One other type of object found in Aquarius is a galaxy. Galaxies are large, connected groups of stars, gases, and planets. Earth is part of the Milky Way galaxy. More than a dozen different galaxies can be seen in Aquarius. One of these is NGC 7252. It is also called the Atoms-for-Peace galaxy. NGC 7252 is actually two galaxies crashing into each other. Its name comes from a 1953 speech given by US President Dwight D. Eisenhower. Its swirling clouds of dust look a little bit like a drawing of an atom.

An atom is the smallest possible piece of something. The Atoms-for-Peace galaxy looks like an atom.

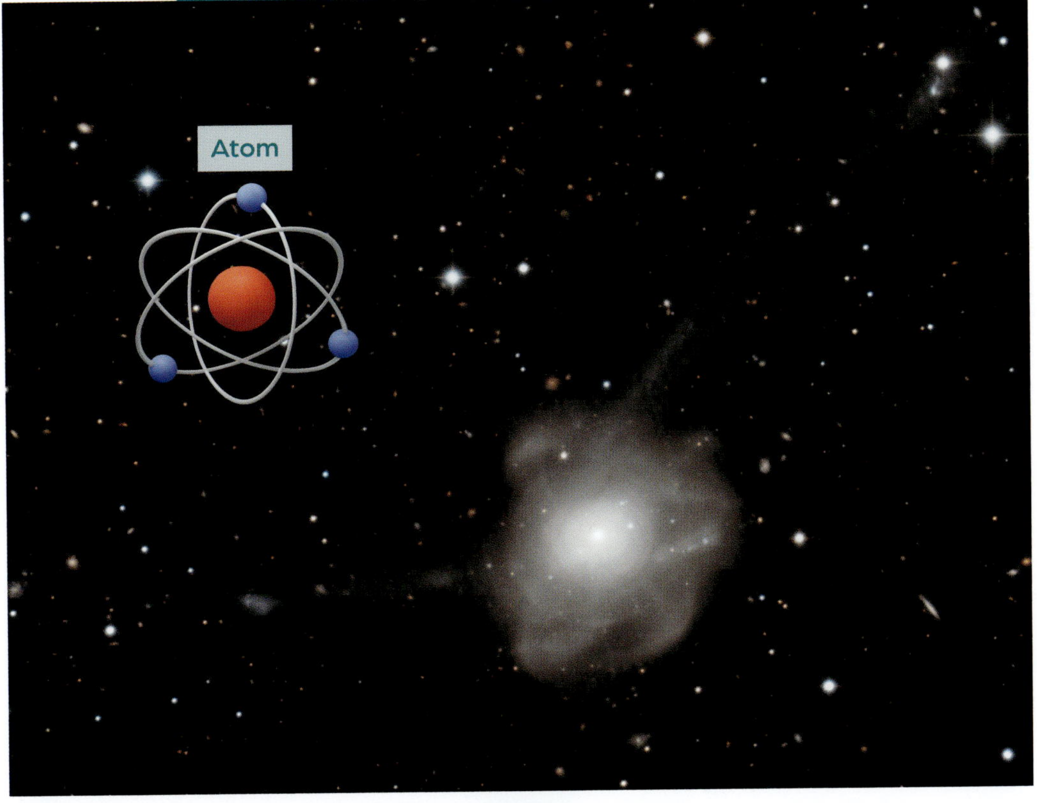

CHAPTER TWO

THE ORIGIN OF THE MYTH

Aquarius has been associated with water for thousands of years. **Ancient** people in the Middle East may have recognized Aquarius as early as 4000 BC. People across the region called Aquarius by names that meant "water bucket" or "water jar." Some cultures saw a person pouring water. Others saw only the jar.

Many of the most well-known constellations were named by the ancient Greeks. The Greco-Roman astronomer Ptolemy (TAH-luh-mee) spent many years studying the stars. Around AD 150, he wrote a book called *The Almagest*. In the book, Ptolemy wrote about the stars and planets. He recorded 48 constellations. Most of these are part of the 88 official constellations today.

Some people see Aquarius as a giant water jug.

OCEAN IN THE SKY

Aquarius is part of a region of the night sky known as the celestial ocean. This region is filled with constellations connected to water. These include Cetus (SEE-tuss) the Whale, Pisces (PY-seez) the Fish, Eridanus (eh-RID-uh-nuss) the River, and Delphinus (dell-FY-nuss) the Dolphin. The constellations in this region are all dim. A dark, clear sky is needed to see them well. Many of the constellations are connected with a great flood in ancient Mesopotamia. The Sun passes through these constellations during the rainy season in the Middle East.

Pisces the Fish is one of the constellations near Aquarius.

Aquarius is connected with the Greek myth of Ganymede (GA-nih-meed). This myth existed for hundreds of years before Ptolemy's writings. The legend of Ganymede first appeared in the famous **epic** poem the *Iliad* by Homer. The *Iliad* was written around the 700s BC.

The Greeks named constellations for famous animals and heroes. The Greek word for constellation is *katasterismoi*. *Katasterismoi* means "placings of the stars." Ancient Greeks believed the stars were placed by the gods. The constellations were used to teach important stories and lessons. Ancient Greeks also used constellations to tell time. Constellations appear in the sky at different times of year. The positions of the constellations marked the time for special events. Constellations also marked the time for planting, plowing, and other farming activities.

CHAPTER THREE

The Story of Aquarius

Ganymede was a shepherd boy. He was the youngest son of Tros. Tros founded the ancient city of Troy. Ganymede was known for his great beauty. One day, Zeus was flying in the air in the form of an eagle. Zeus was the king of the gods. He saw Ganymede tending a flock of sheep. Zeus was stunned by Ganymede's beauty. He decided Ganymede should live with the gods on Mount Olympus. Zeus swooped down and snatched Ganymede. Zeus carried him up into the sky.

Zeus kidnapped Ganymede because he was drawn to the young man's beauty.

Ganymede served Zeus and the other gods.

In Olympus, Ganymede became the official cupbearer of the gods. It was his job to serve drinks. He would live with the gods and never die. But some of the gods were angry about his position. Hebe (HEE-bee) used to be the cupbearer. She was the goddess of youth. She was also Zeus and Hera's daughter. Hera was the queen of the gods. Ganymede had replaced Hebe in the important role. Hera was not happy. She also thought Zeus paid too much attention to Ganymede. But the other gods liked Ganymede. Zeus decided to place him in the sky in a position of honor. Ganymede became the constellation Aquarius. Up in the night sky, he poured out heavenly water forever.

Zeus gave Ganymede's family a special gift to apologize for taking Ganymede. In some stories, Zeus gave them horses that would live forever. In others, he gave a golden vine.

THE ZODIAC

Aquarius is one of 12 original zodiac constellations. The zodiac is an imaginary belt around the sky. It follows the path of the Sun throughout the year. This path is known as the ecliptic. More than 2,000 years ago, ancient Babylonians divided the ecliptic path into twelve regions. Each region belongs to a different constellation. Aquarius covers January 20 through February 18. Someone born in this time period is called an Aquarius. Some of the other zodiac constellations include Gemini, Leo, and Libra. Many of the zodiac constellations are animals. Because of this, the ancient Greeks called the zodiac the *zōdiakos kyklos*. This means "circle of animals."

The start and end dates of a zodiac period can change from year to year due to the position of the Sun and Earth. For example, some people born on June 21 are considered Geminis, and some are considered Cancers.

CHAPTER FOUR

The Myth of Aquarius in Other Cultures

The Greeks were not the only ancient people studying the sky. People around the world watched the stars and created their own stories. In many areas, the constellation Aquarius is connected to water. This is probably because in many parts of the world, Aquarius is visible in the sky during the rainy season.

In some of the earliest **civilizations** in the Middle East, Aquarius was seen as a jar pouring out the Tigris (TY-griss) and Euphrates (yoo-FRAY-teez) rivers. In ancient Egypt, Aquarius was believed to be Hapi (HAH-pee), the god of the Nile River. Each year, Hapi would cause the river to flood. The flood was seen as a blessing. The Nile's floods helped crops grow.

Hapi represented the Nile's yearly flood. These floods made the land good for farming.

The snake-tortoise guardian is called Genbu in Japan and Hyeonmu in Korea.

In Arabic legends, Aquarius is known as the well bucket. Many of the stars in Aquarius have names connected with the word *luck* in Arabic. This may be due to Aquarius's connection with the rainy season. The rainy season was known as a time of good fortune.

In China, Aquarius is part of a large tortoise constellation called Xuanwu (shee-AHN-woo), or the Black Tortoise. The Black Tortoise is one of four guardian animals representing different directions. The Black Tortoise represents the north. It is also connected with winter and the element of water. The constellation is sometimes shown as a snake-tortoise **warrior** that guards the north.

CHAPTER FIVE

How to Find Aquarius in the Sky

Aquarius is a large constellation. But it can be difficult to find. People should avoid **light pollution** when looking for Aquarius. A clear, dark night is best.

The best time to see Aquarius is October and November. During these months, Aquarius is higher in the sky. In the Northern **Hemisphere**, Aquarius can be seen in the southern sky. In the Southern Hemisphere, it can be found in the northern sky or straight overhead.

After waiting for a clear night, find the ecliptic. Look at the location of the Sun during sunset. Then connect it to the rising Moon. The imaginary line between them is the ecliptic.

The Moon is a helpful tool to find the ecliptic. But a full Moon can make it difficult to stargaze, especially with fainter constellations such as Aquarius. Planets will always be near the ecliptic line. People can also keep track of the Sun's path during the day to find the ecliptic.

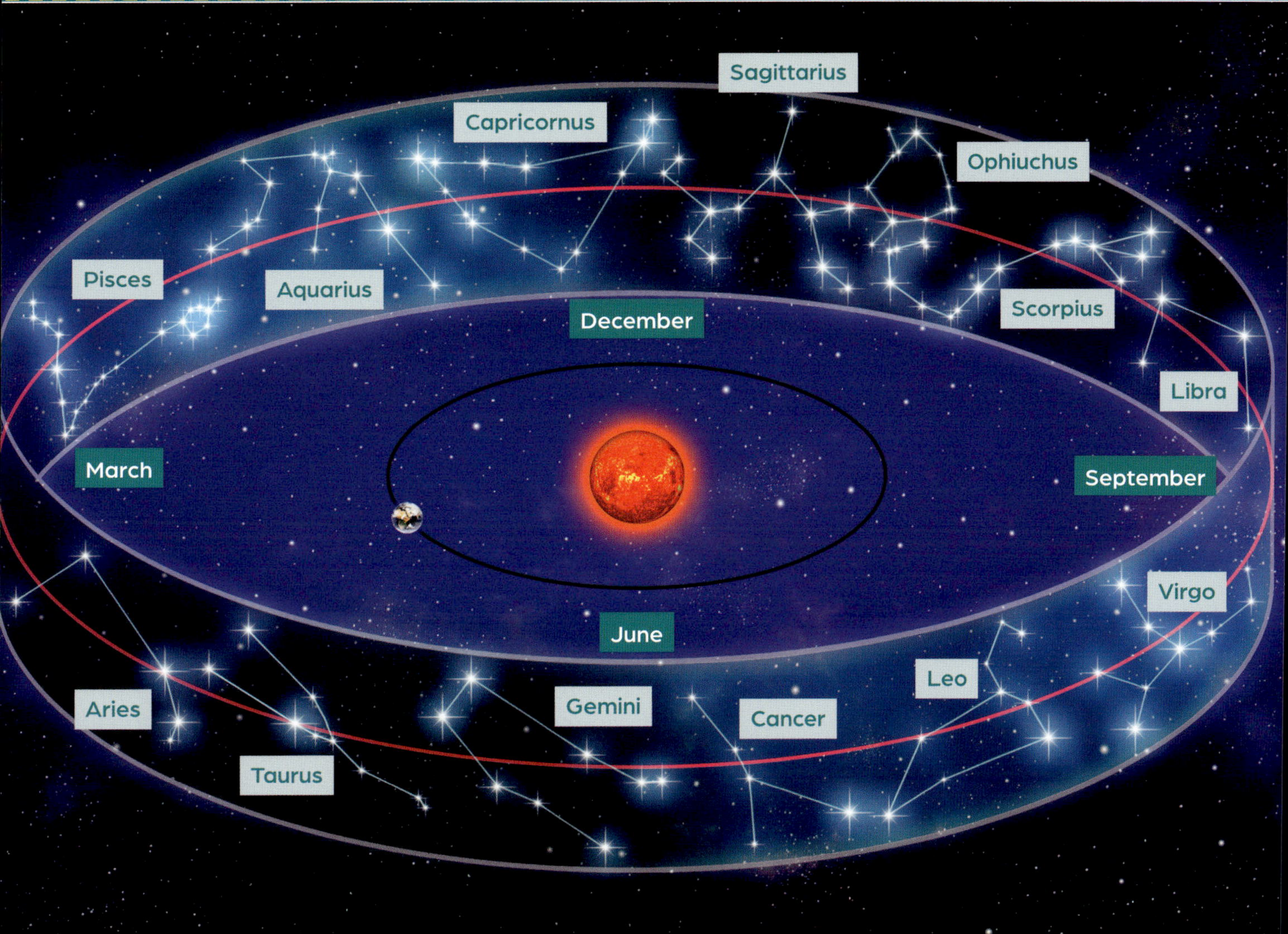

A thirteenth constellation called Ophiuchus also lies on the ecliptic. The Babylonians did not include it in their zodiac, so most people today do not recognize it as part of the zodiac.

TIPS FOR BACKYARD ASTRONOMERS

The most important tools for stargazing are patience and curiosity. Many objects in the sky can be enjoyed using only the eyes. Other tools such as binoculars and star charts can also be useful. With binoculars, a person can see craters on the Moon. Star charts show what objects can be found in different areas of the sky. A tool called a planisphere shows which constellations are visible at different times of the year. Astronomy apps may also help with locating constellations. But looking at phones and other screens can make stargazing difficult. Most experts recommend not using electronic devices so people's eyes can get used to the dark. It may be best to consult apps or other electronic sources before a night of stargazing.

Telescopes also help people look at space objects. But they are more difficult to use than binoculars and usually cost more.

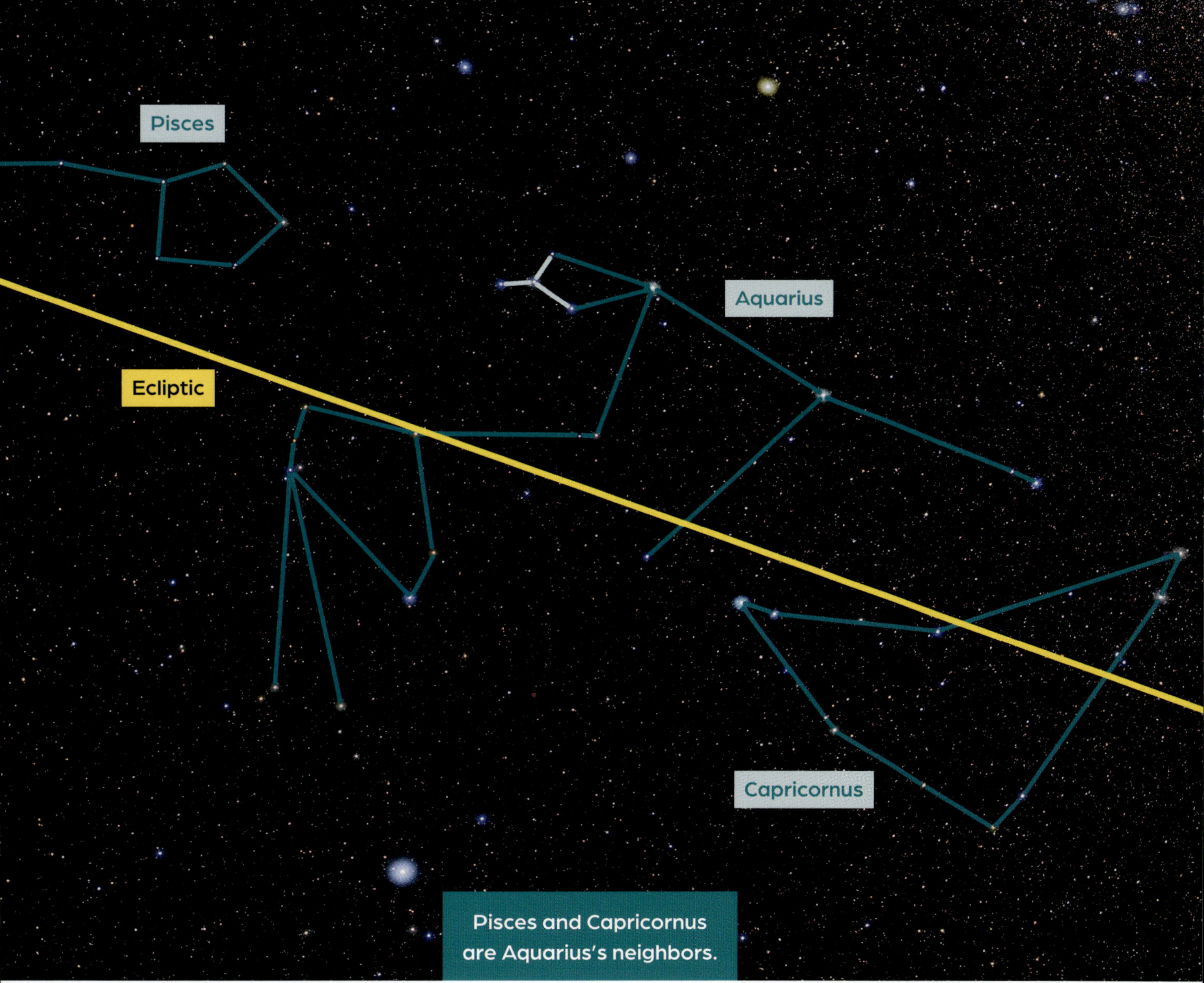

Pisces and Capricornus are Aquarius's neighbors.

Other constellations along the ecliptic can help stargazers find Aquarius. One nearby constellation is Capricornus. It is easier to find. Capricornus has a triangle shape and bright stars. It is right under Aquarius. After finding Capricornus, look for the Y-shaped Water Jar asterism. It can guide viewers to the rest of the constellation.

GLOSSARY

ancient (AYN-shunt) Something that is ancient is very old or belongs to times long ago. The ancient Greeks told the story of Ganymede.

astronomical (a-struh-NAH-mih-kull) Something astronomical has to do with astronomy, the study of stars and other objects in space. The International Astronomical Union determined the 88 official constellations.

atmosphere (AT-muss-feer) An atmosphere is the layer of gases that surrounds a planet. Meteors burn in Earth's atmosphere.

celestial (seh-LESS-chull) Something celestial has to do with the sky. The stars and constellations are celestial objects.

civilizations (si-vuh-lih-ZAY-shunz) Civilizations are complex societies with laws and culture. Many ancient civilizations practiced astronomy.

debris (duh-BREE) Debris is made up of pieces of things that have been destroyed or broken down. Meteor showers happen when space debris burns up in Earth's atmosphere.

epic (EH-pik) An epic is a long story in the form of a poem, usually describing the adventures of a hero. The *Iliad* is an epic by Homer.

hemisphere (HEH-mih-sfeer) A hemisphere is half of a sphere. Earth is divided into the Northern Hemisphere and Southern Hemisphere.

light pollution (LYT puh-LOO-shun) Light pollution is the light caused by artificial lights such as streetlights that makes it difficult to see the sky. It is difficult to see Aquarius in areas with light pollution.

nebulae (NEH-byoo-lee) Nebulae are clouds of gas and dust in space where stars are born. The Saturn Nebula is one of the nebulae in Aquarius.

warrior (WOR-ee-uhr) A warrior is a soldier. Chinese astronomers saw Aquarius as part of a warrior who guarded the north.

FAST FACTS

- Constellations are groupings of stars in the sky that form pictures. Stars are glowing balls of gas throughout the universe. The Sun is a star.
- Aquarius is a constellation known as the Water Bearer. It is one of the oldest and largest constellations.
- Many space objects can be found within Aquarius. These include globular clusters, nebulae, and galaxies.
- The legend of Aquarius is based on the story of Zeus and Ganymede. Ganymede was a handsome boy chosen as the cupbearer of the gods.
- Other cultures have their own legends about Aquarius. In ancient Egypt, Aquarius was a god that floods the Nile River. In China, Aquarius is part of a giant snake-tortoise guardian.
- Aquarius can be found on clear nights by using nearby stars as guides.

ONE STRIDE FURTHER

- Why do you think people imagined shapes and stories in the stars?
- What story would you imagine if you were the first to see the constellation Aquarius?
- Why was the rainy season so important to ancient people? How is water still important today?

FIND OUT MORE

IN THE LIBRARY

Read, John A. *A Kid's Guide to the Night Sky: Simple Ways to Explore the Universe*. Naperville, IL: Sourcebooks, 2024.

Sabol, Stephanie. *Where Are the Constellations?* New York, NY: Penguin Workshop, 2021.

Ventura, Marne. *Meteor Showers*. Parker, CO: The Child's World, 2025.

ON THE WEB

Visit our website for links about Aquarius:

childsworld.com/links

Note to Parents, Caregivers, Teachers, and Librarians: We routinely verify our web links to make sure they are safe and active sites. So encourage your readers to check them out!

INDEX